The Galaxies
in Mars

Venus [Zohreh Golkari]

Kidsocado Publishing House
Vancouver, Canada

Phone : +1 (833) 633 8654
WhatsApp: +1 (236) 333 7248
Email: info@kidsocado.com
https://kidsocadopublishinghouse.com

Serial Number: P2346250136

Title: The Galaxies in Mars

Author: Venus [Zohreh Golkari]

Illustrator: Zeynab Mohajeri

ISBN: 978-1-990760-92-1

Metadata: Junior Fiction, Aeronautics, Astronautics & Space Science

Book Format: Paperback

Pages: 28

Canada Publish Date: June 2023

Publisher: Kidsocado Publishing House

To my Dear Nieces:

Baran & Rosha & Shamim & Nila

&

To my Dear Nephews:

Parham & Shayan

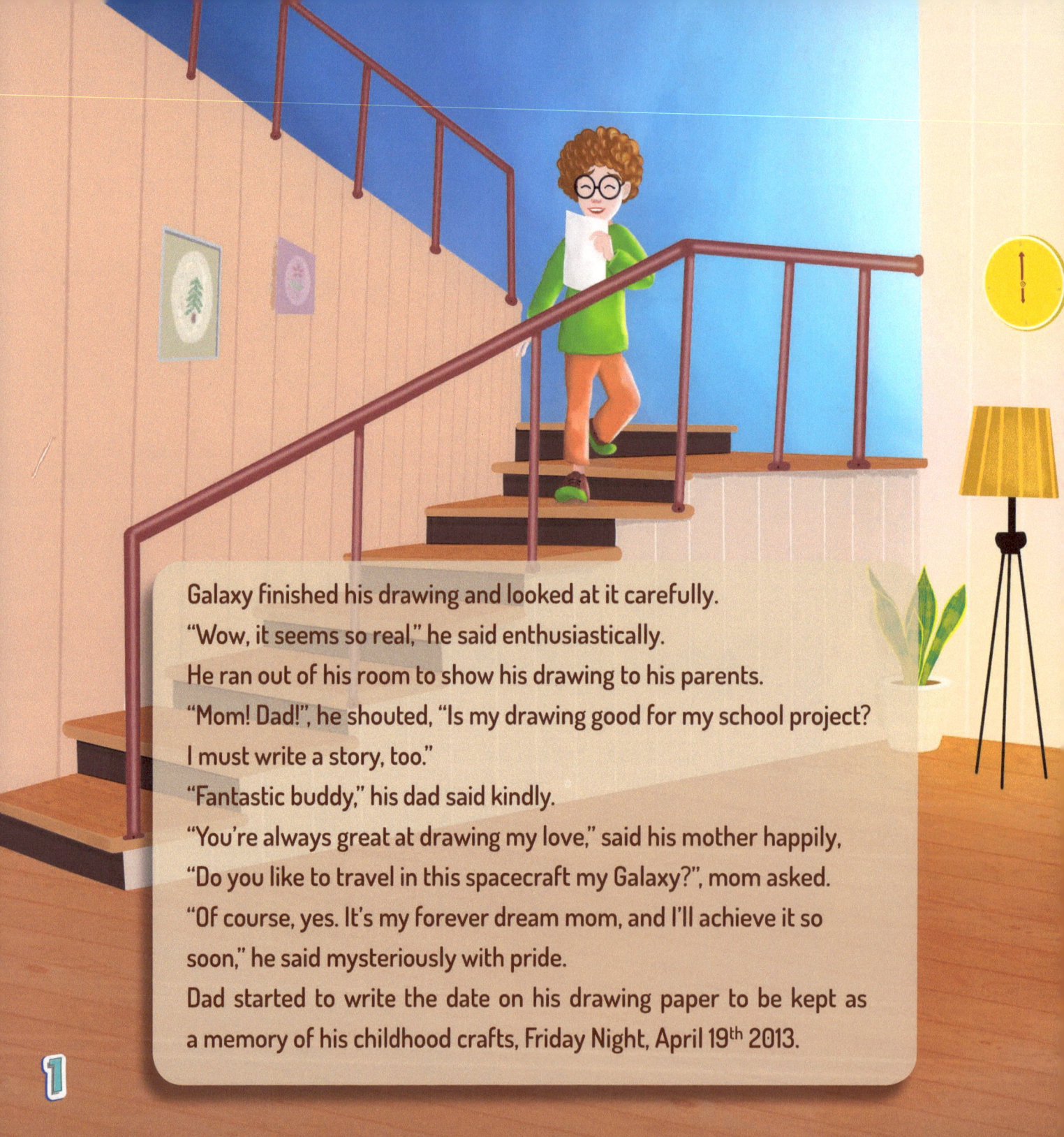

Galaxy finished his drawing and looked at it carefully.

"Wow, it seems so real," he said enthusiastically.

He ran out of his room to show his drawing to his parents.

"Mom! Dad!", he shouted, "Is my drawing good for my school project? I must write a story, too."

"Fantastic buddy," his dad said kindly.

"You're always great at drawing my love," said his mother happily, "Do you like to travel in this spacecraft my Galaxy?", mom asked.

"Of course, yes. It's my forever dream mom, and I'll achieve it so soon," he said mysteriously with pride.

Dad started to write the date on his drawing paper to be kept as a memory of his childhood crafts, Friday Night, April 19th 2013.

After spending a nice evening with his nice parents, Galaxy said good night, and went towards his room just by starring at the spacecraft of his drawing. He was sitting behind his desk, took a pencil to add something on the paper, but wasn't sure what. He thought about a background for the spacecraft and the creation of some aliens.

"I've never thought about how aliens look like," he said to himself, "what color are they? Green? blue? or maybe red? I think they should have more than two hands, they can have horns, too." While he was imagining and thinking deeply, suddenly he noticed something on the paper, a strange creature he had never seen. A red alien with round big head, two big eyes, three small horns, oval-shaped body and four hands, two small, two normal.

Open-mouthed with round eyes, Galaxy just gazed at the paper. The alien was starting to move on the paper, like an animation. It went towards the spacecraft and said, "Hey boy, what's your name? I'm Neon."

Galaxy was completely shocked, he tried to say something, but it was really difficult. He had a feeling of fear and excitement.

"Galaxy", he replied astonishingly and asked, "Who are you? What are you doing here? How did you get here?"

Neon laughed calmly and said, "Galaxy, I'm your friend, you shouldn›t be afraid of me, I came here to fulfill your wish."

"My wish ?!", Galaxy asked and continued, "how do you know what my wish is."

"I know for sure," he replied kindly," I can take you to my wonderful land with your spacecraft and show you my own planet, the red one, have you ever heard about it?"

"Mars?! Oh, noooo! Incredible!" he said.

"Exactly, it's the reason that my skin is red and my family is from a special race, Neonism, our color is neon, if you turn off the light, you can find me easily, so I'm not good for hide and seek bud." Neon laughed ....

Neon took Galaxy's hand and pulled him into the paper. It seemed Galaxy dived into the paper and disappeared.

He found himself into the spacecraft. There was a lot of equipment and thousand lights and buttons. Neon explained to him how to wear the space costume and gave some necessary tips on how to walk in the space. After a while, the spacecraft stopped and the door opened. Such an unbelievable feeling he had!

Neon said, "here is my hometown, can you guess where it is, Galaxy?"

"It must be Mars, based on the red color of the atmosphere," Galaxy answered wisely.

" You're really intelligent Buddy," Neon said and continued," come with me, I'll show you the whole planet and how we live here."

The atmosphere wasn't as clear as something Galaxy had expected. Because he compared it with the earth's. It seemed that everywhere was full of dust, and everywhere had the theme of red, the atmosphere, the land, everywhere he saw. They walked all through the red planet. Their houses were like semi-circle and more interestingly, the houses were smart, they talked to it and ordered what they needed such as opening the door or preparing food, turning on the TV and the other tasks like these. Their life style was extremely amusing for Galaxy especially their food!

When Galaxy saw their food, he couldn't control himself and burst into laughter.

Neon was shocked, just stared at him and asked, " why are you laughing? What's wrong with our food?"

Galaxy asked curiously, " How do you feel full with such a little food?"

"They're enough boy, you can try, then you see," Neon said then asked, "now what would you like to eat?"

Galaxy replied reluctantly, " I don't know the name of your food."

Neon said," the same as yours because our ancestors learned from the earth's residents what the food is and they made some necessary changes to be compatible with our taste. I think you might like pizza."

"Pizza?!," Galaxy asked surprisingly, "do you know what pizza is and you have the real one?!"

"Of course we have," Neon replied confidently, let's go to a famous pizzeria on Mars, *Neo_Pizza_Hut.*

Galaxy burst out laughing. "Are you kidding me, boy?" he said.

"No, no, believe me!", Neon said.

After all of these excitements they ordered Martian pizza with tomato and basil topping. Galaxy couldn't wait to eat this pizza, he was really hungry, but he was so surprised. He gazed at his plate, there were some tiny white, green and red triangles!

"How interesting, is it really pizza?!" He laughed and asked surprisingly.

"Yes! You must know it well," It said.

Enter

Neo_pizza_Hut

Trying the alien's food was one of the most amazing experiences he had in his trip.

"It is the time to return home, my parents must have been worried for my absence, actually it's the first time I left the house without their permission, you know kids should always tell their parents where they go", Galaxy explained.

Neon whispered to itself mysteriously, "Hope they didn't have to worry so much about him."

They returned to the spacecraft and headed back to Galaxy's drawing. In a blink of an eye Galaxy found himself in his room, but it seemed strange.

Galaxy started to asked continuously, "Is it really my room?! How has my room's design been changed since last night?!!! OMG!

My bed is different, oh, look at my telescope, why it's packed?! Where are all my space posters on the wall? These aren't my books on the desk. Neon, are you still there, I'm completely confused."

Neon replied quietly from the inside of the paper, "Yes but, I think I know what happened."

14

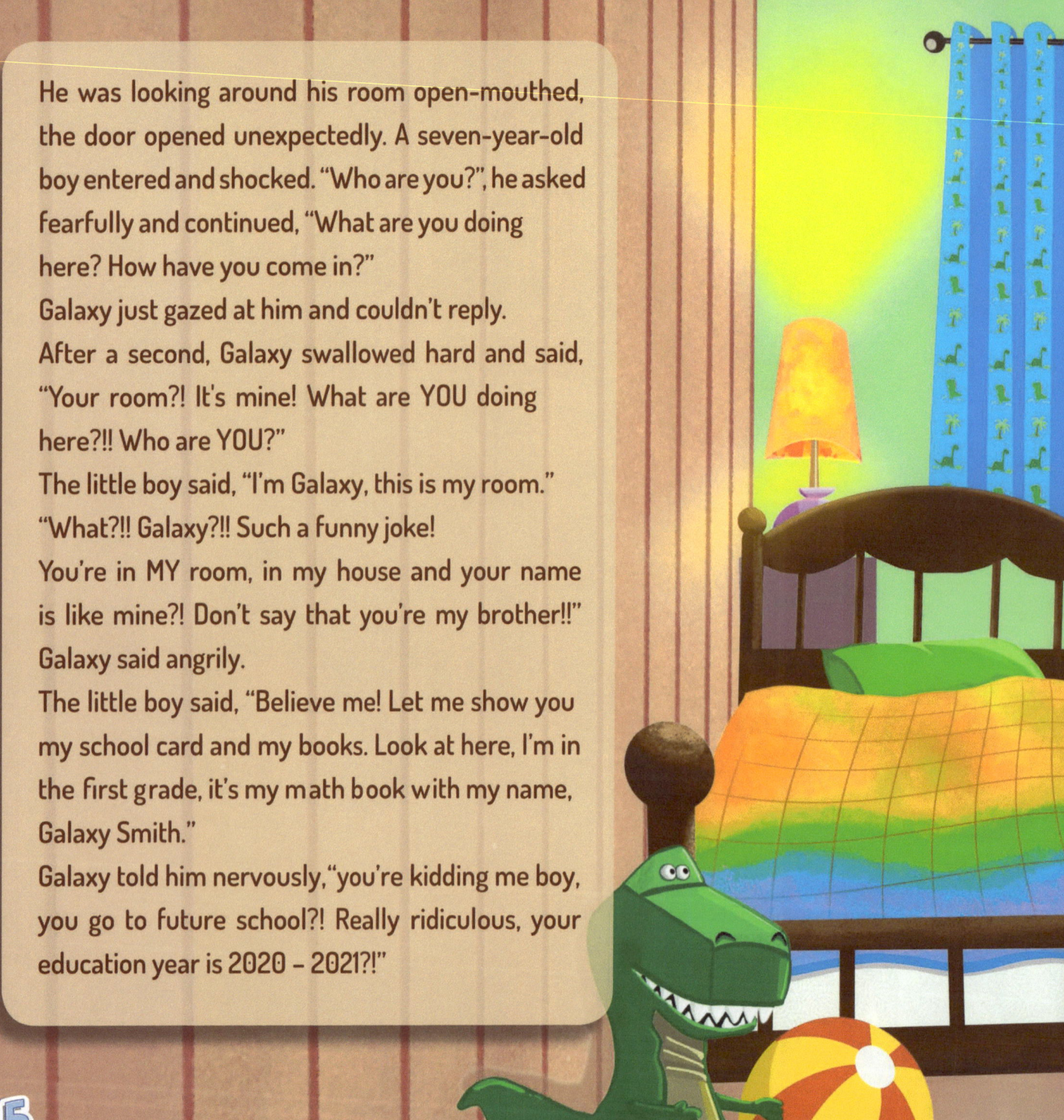

He was looking around his room open-mouthed, the door opened unexpectedly. A seven-year-old boy entered and shocked. "Who are you?", he asked fearfully and continued, "What are you doing here? How have you come in?"

Galaxy just gazed at him and couldn't reply.

After a second, Galaxy swallowed hard and said, "Your room?! It's mine! What are YOU doing here?!! Who are YOU?"

The little boy said, "I'm Galaxy, this is my room."

"What?!! Galaxy?!! Such a funny joke!

You're in MY room, in my house and your name is like mine?! Don't say that you're my brother!!" Galaxy said angrily.

The little boy said, "Believe me! Let me show you my school card and my books. Look at here, I'm in the first grade, it's my math book with my name, Galaxy Smith."

Galaxy told him nervously, "you're kidding me boy, you go to future school?! Really ridiculous, your education year is 2020 – 2021?!"

To make a long story short, Galaxy's trip took about seven years, according to the earth's time. After he disappeared his family couldn't find him and they were so sad and demolished completely. His parents decided to have another baby to fill the void after their son's disappearance. Since the baby was a boy, in honor of their first son, they named him GALAXY.

18

A. Check True (T) or False (F)

1. Galaxy is interested in space a lot. ....

2. He had already drawn an alien. ....

3. The alien has three small hands. ....

4. Neon›s skin is red because Mars is too hot. ....

5. Neon pulled Galaxy into the paper. ....

6. Neon›s hometown is Mars. ....

7. The Aliens' life style was fancy for Galaxy. ....

8. Galaxy was not impressed by their Martian Pizza. ....

9. When Galaxy returned, there were a big change in his room. ....

10. The little boy was Galaxy's brother. ....

B. Answer the following questions.

1. What was Galaxy's forever dream?

2. When did he draw the picture?

3. Why did he draw the picture?

4. Had he drawn any background for the space craft, before he showed it to his parents?

5. Why the alien's name was Neon?

6. What did he feel when he saw Neon on the paper?

7. Why did Neon come to his house?

8. How were their houses in Mars?

9. What was the name of the most famous pizzeria in Mars?

10. Was Galaxy's room unchanged after he came back?

ANSWER KEY

Part A :

1. T
2. F
3. F
4. F
5. T
6. T
7. T
8. F
9. T
10. T

Part B:

1. His forever dream was travelling to space.
2. He drew the picture on Friday, 19th of April 2013.
3. He drew the picture for his school project.
4. No, he hadn't.
5. Because he was from the special race, Neonism.
6. He had the feeling of fear and excitement.
7. Neon came to his house to fulfil Galaxy's desire.
8. They were semi-circle and smart houses.
9. Its name was *Neo_Pizza_Hut*.
10. No, it wasn't. It changed a lot.

Another book by this author

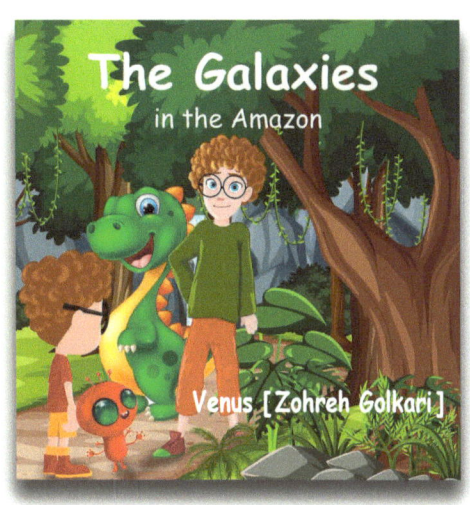

Scan this Code:

Other Books from This Publishing House

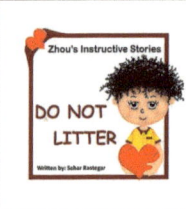 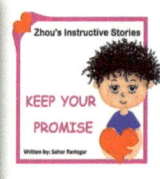 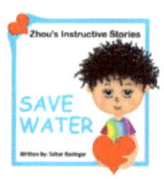 

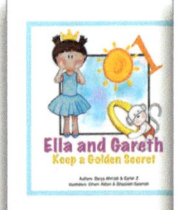  

Access here:

www.ingramcontent.com/pod-product-compliance
Lightning Source LLC
Chambersburg PA
CBHW041608120626
46551CB00002B/358